I0765790

THE ROOTS OF HUMAN CIRCUMSTANCE

RAYMOND A. HULT

Order this book online at www.trafford.com
or email orders@trafford.com

Most Trafford titles are also available at major online book retailers.

Print information available on the last page.

ISBN: 978-1-6987-0534-7 (sc)
ISBN: 978-1-6987-0532-3 (hc)
ISBN: 978-1-6987-0533-0 (e)

Library of Congress Control Number: 2021900415

Trafford rev. 01/07/2020

www.trafford.com
North America & international
toll-free: 844-688-6899 (USA & Canada)
fax: 812 355 4082

CONTENTS

PREFACE

Mortality begins at birth and is immediately impacted by what will become a long string of circumstances determining the quality of life's journey for however long it exists. It's different for everybody. For the lucky few, life becomes a totally satisfying experience with few bumps in the road. For those less fortunate, it can result in a miserable experience from beginning to end. For the rest of us, it lies somewhere in between.

The motive for writing this book has been to highlight some of the major causes or roots determining the circumstances facing the mortal saga. Some destructive roots for the most part can't be avoided although in some cases minimized. Others are mostly up to each human to avoid or suffer the dire circumstances.

Beneficial roots similarly impact humans in a couple of ways. For some, they take hold with little or no effort on behalf of the recipient. For others, the good roots don't magically materialize and must be initiated by the recipient to result in a positive outcome.

Hopefully, readers will be assisted in recognizing and minimizing the bad and capitalizing on the good.

ONE

BIBLICAL ORIGIN

Trying to figure out the circumstances determining one's human life experience starts with attempting to ascertain its origin. There's really only a couple of theorized possibilities that result in pitting religion against science.

Although there may be others, the most universally accepted religious explanation is found in the Bible from which I'll devote the remainder of this chapter. I'll consider the scientific theory in chapter 2.

The Bible doesn't waste any time in devoting its First Book of Moses called Genesis to explaining how the Earth was formed along with the first two humans, Adam and Eve. Accepting that would of course mean fully formed humans much the same as exist today originated in that form. There have been no intermediate versions. Fully formed physical bodies and mental capability have continued essentially unabated from the beginning.

Moses allegedly received that revelation directly from God. The problem I have with that is there is no available evidence anything like that ever happened. It could just have easily been some fictitious story make up by a mere human. There's no way at this late date to put Moses on the witness stand or to find other witnesses who may have been able to authenticate or discard his account.

One way of determining the credibility of Adam and Eve originating humanity is to evaluate the believability of the creation of earth as outlined in Genesis. Not very convincing to say the least.

Moses records God created light on the first day, but didn't get around to creating the sun and the moon until the fourth day. What was the source of the light for the first three?

Then, God created grass, herbs and fruit bearing trees on the third day, but there was no sun until the fourth. How could those plants grow without the sun? It's hard to conceive of plants existing in frigid conditions. Wouldn't an intelligent creator want to create the sun first?

The sceptic I am, if God created the sun on the fourth day and the earth already existed although "without form and void," it makes me wonder what that mass was rotating around in the meantime. Again, seems to me the sun needs to exist as the first step in any creative effort.

Genesis records that the firmament (universe) was created on the second day. Why was a creative effort that enormous a necessary element in the creation of the earth? Yes, the sun and the moon were necessary, but why everything else we now know exists in an ever-expanding universe?

The known universe is currently estimated to contain over 100 billion galaxies with a total of roughly 10 billion trillion stars. The sun is just one of those stars. As every minute goes by, it's estimated the universe is continuing to increase its volume by a trillion cubic light-years (the distance it takes light to ravel in a year-cubed) with no end in sight. Note: The speed of light travels approximately 670,7 million miles/hr. x 24 hrs./ day x 365 days/yr. = # miles light travels in a year.

The point is the credibility of Adam and Eve being the first human beings originally created much the same in body and mind as humans today must be evaluated alongside the credibility of the same source of information relating to the Genesis account of the creation of the earth. Add to that in chapter 3 of Genesis the account of Lucifer in the form of a talking snake and my doubt doesn't seem that farfetched.

Then comes the question of how a supposedly perfect creator could have created humans so imperfectly. The human body is admittedly an amazing personage in form and capability, but there's a lot that leaves to be desired. Why create Adam and eve with body parts so inferior to non-human animal life. For example; the ability to see better, hear better, smell better etc. etc... Wouldn't you think a perfect creative entity would have endowed humans with the superior capabilities.

A significant percentage of the earth's population at any one time suffers from incapacitating ailments attributable to a multitude of different maladies. Why create bodies so different in capability to resist infirmity and brains so different in the ability to successfully face the challenges of humanity.

In trying to determine how humans have ended up so uniquely dissimilar over thousands of years, the biblical explanation makes it difficult to rationalize the result. If the biblical explanation is correct, you would think most of humanity would have remained genetically similar to Adam and Eve. Since that obviously hasn't been the case, it calls into question the origination account supposedly revealed to and promoted by Moses.

TWO

SCIENTIFIC ORIGIN

Acknowledging up front my agnostic skepticism of any divine revelation, I favor the scientific over the religious explanation for the origin of man. It just makes more sense to me even though there's no way beyond a shadow of a doubt to know exactly how we've ended up like we are.

Although impossible for my mind to fully comprehend, I trust scientists who claim that, over 13 billion years ago, an incomprehensible physical event occurred that initiated the creation of an ever-expanding universe some refer to as The Big Bang Theory. The result has been the creation of 95% dark matter and energy and the remaining 5% consisting of planets, stars and galaxies, the enormity of which were described in chapter 1.

The earth and the sun around which it now rotates were part of the 5%. It's estimated the earth came into existence about 4.54 billion years ago. Oceans formed about a half a billion years later. The earliest appearance of life occurred not long after the formation of the oceans identified as simple microorganisms created in hydrothermal vent precipitates

From the origination of life on earth, the variations have become increasingly complex from one generation to the next. I tend to attribute that to the survival of the fittest as promoted by Charles Darwin in his books entitled *On the Origin of Species* (1859) and *The Decent of Man* (1871). Human evolution eventually developed from now extinct primates dating back millions of years ago.

The human lineage progressed from Australopithecus to Homo habilis to Homo erectus to Homo neanderthalensis and finally to Homo sapiens. It's theorized humans first evolved in Africa about 315,000 years ago.

For evolution to take effect requires long periods of time for significant physical and mental alterations to occur. These incremental changes are due to minute genetic modifications from generation to generation. Positive cellular variations provide recipients with the best chance of progressing to the next generation. Those without such benefit or who inherit negative adaptations fall by the wayside and often disappear from continuing to reproduce their inferior genetic variety.

Physical surroundings have reportedly played a significant role in the survival of the fittest. Cellular adaptations that can best survive in a particular environment favor those possessing such modifications over those not so fortunate in the constant battle to successfully progress from one generation to the next.

In trying to explain the circumstances of how humanity has turned out like it has, I side on the scientific theory of the decent of man over the biblical account. That's because it seems the only logical explanation of how we have ended up with the vast difference of human variety including skin/ hair/eye color, mental capacity and all the other differences in genetic makeup.

There's no doubt a significant cause determining the circumstances we end up in has to do with the human environment we inhabit. However, we can't deny the other significant root is the DNA we've been blessed or burdened with at birth. The cause of those differences can only be credibly explained by the scientific theory of evolution and the constant minute alteration of genes from generation to generation over hundreds of thousands of years. Relying on the explanation in Genesis simply doesn't account for that magnitude of vast diversity.

THREE

RACISM

I grew up in Utah around very few black people and so any concern about racism was mostly non-existent It rarely crossed my mind. Now, I realize that was not the case in a large segment of America. Researchers have counted almost 4000 black people killed in "racial terror lynchings" in a dozen Southern states between 1877 and 1950.

I was born in 1943 and had no idea. Now I know, well into the 1950s, Blacks were refused seats in restaurants and rooms in hotels. They were forced to the back of buses and refused drinking from "white only" water fountains. Their housing was restricted to the wrong side of the tracks.

I laughed with others in Utah when my dad and some friends made their faces black and sang songs mimicking a disrespectful version of black verbiage. There was a restaurant nearby with a huge face of a black man where you walked through the mouth to enter. It was called The Coon Chicken Inn. I failed to considered it may be offensive.

It wasn't until I was stationed in Los Angeles as a Special Agent with the FBI that I spent a lot of time in South LA occupied almost entirely by black families just barely scratching by to put food on the table. It hit me for the first time that racism had taken a horrible toll on a minority still trying to recover from a racist past dating back to earliest America when slavery was a significant part of the American fabric.

It was later in the 1980s when I was transferred to Tyler, Texas that a degree of racism was still alive and flourishing. The black community was isolated to a designated section of town. There was a yearly fair with Thursdays designated for the Blacks to attend. Most didn't venture to attend during the remaining days of the week. I mostly just ignored jokes by my homegrown friends when using the N word in an effort to elicit a laugh.

Racism in 2020 was still raising its ugly head. During my 27 years in law enforcement, I'd estimate the vast majority of local policemen and sheriff deputies were a credit to their profession. There were, however, a few I ran into who exhibited troubling racist attitudes and didn't deserve the badge they were wearing.

The George Floyd incident was a prime example of police racism as he was brutally choked to death by a Minneapolis, Minnesota officer as his fellow officers stood idly by. Black Lives Matter demonstrations exploded across the country demanding an end to disrespecting and mistreating men and women simply because of the color of their skin.

I've brought up racism because it provides a good explanation of the human circumstance Blacks and other minorities have been forced to endure. I try to put myself in their situation and wonder how different my life would have played out had I found myself with their color of skin. I'm certain my life would have ended up significantly different.

Picturing myself living in a high rise dilapidated rental building on the wrong side of town with a single mother working two low paying jobs to barely get by would have made me a totally different child. Being enrolled in inferior schools with the fear of gangs an ever-present danger would have retarded by development as a model citizen. Being extremely poor would have tempted me to deal drugs as the only alternative to get by financially. It's a lot easier to say you could have made the best of a bad deal until you're the one actually trying to navigate the bad deal.

Redirecting the subject, a bit, I've often wondered why Blacks in general are more physically capable than me. That has become obvious being 6'4" tall and never capable of dunking a basketball. This is where I hypothesize bringing DNA into the spotlight. Is it because Blacks had it harder in Africa surviving all the different obstacles my ancestors didn't have to live through? Therefore, only the hardiest with their superior DNA moved forward from one generation to the next. Only those who could run the fastest, jump the highest with the most muscular frames survived.

That has now resulted in the best athletes being Black while making a lot of money and living the life of the wealthy elite.

So, that makes for an interesting contradiction. Poor blacks that don't become star athletes and end up growing up in poverty end up with lives opposite of those who benefit financially based on the superiority of their inherited genes. Thus, the circumstances of how Blacks negotiate life can be diametrically diverse even while inheriting the same skin color.

I can only hope America is finally turning the corner on destructive racist ideology with factions like the KKK and White Supremist movements becoming nothing more than a past despicable page in our nation's history. I don't see it happening while I'm still alive, but maybe later during the lives of my children and grandchildren. Hopefully, the color of skin will soon one day have ceased to determine a negative situation of one's life experience.

FOUR

FAITH

Not being a religious true believer myself, I've had numerous opportunities discussing various doctrines espoused by those who are. Unable to furnish credible evidence to support their resolute beliefs, some of these die-hard advocates have fallen back on their faith as sustaining their absolute conviction beyond a shadow of a doubt.

Faith is defined as "unquestioning belief that does not require proof or evidence." The result is debating the accuracy of such belief is a dead end. Faith alone is often sufficient to dismiss any possibility of a heart-felt dogma being flawed.

The only remaining questions for me is how faith influences the circumstances of the type of lives such die-hard adherents end up living. Does it result in positive or negative outcomes? Does the truth really matter as long as the quality of life is enriched? On the other hand, what are the potential perils?

Thinking about it and trying to be fair, I've come to the conclusion that even if not representing the truth, fervent faith can result in both an upside and a downside. Regardless, an irrefutable reality is it often determines a person's lot in life. It helps explain why a significant part of their life experience turns out like it does.

Those critical of the negative power of faith point to the evil resulting from the Christian Inquisition when hundreds of thousands of blameless non-believers were tortured and killed during the 11th through the 18th centuries. The circumstance surrounding their lives was clearly determined by, in this case, their lack of faith. The life experience for those who committed the torture and murder was likewise determined by a horribly misguided faith.

Historians distinguish four different manifestations of Inquisitions including the Medieval (1184-1230s), the Spanish (1478-1834), the Portuguese (1536-1821), and the Roman (1542-1860). I won't take the time here to detail the catastrophic inhumanity resulting from those whose demented faith convinced them they were righteously endowed with the mission of annihilating those who believed otherwise. Wow! That's several decades where misguided faith resulted in the circumstance of how the lives of millions were hideously impacted.

Those obsessed with absolute faith in numerous religious cults embody a downside adversely affecting lives and explaining the circumstances of how lives have ended up in a devastating downward spiral. Why they ended up living lives of such unconscionable grief and premature death doesn't say much for the faith they blindly chose to embody.

In his book, *The End of Faith*, Sam Harris chronicles the destructive side of fervent faith explaining how dogmatic extremists end up living a catastrophic lifestyle. He points to "The recent conflicts in Palestine (Jews v. Muslims), The Balkans (Orthodox Serbians v. Catholic Croatians; Orthodox Serbians v. Bosnian and Albanian Muslims), Northern Ireland (Protestants v. Catholics), Kashmir (Muslims v. Hindus), Sudan (Muslims v. Christians and Animists), Nigeria (Muslims

v. Christians), Ethiopia and Eritrea (Muslims v. Christians), Sri Lanka (Sinhalese Buddhists v. Tamil Hindus), Indonesia (Muslims v. Timorese Christians), and the Caucasus (Orthodox Russians v. Chechen Muslims; Muslim Azerbaijanis v. Catholic and Orthodox Armenians)."

Unlike the cold war between the United States and other nuclear capable national foes where neither side wants to risk their own annihilation, there now exist Muslim terrorists like ISIS who, if they could get their hands on nuclear weaponry, wouldn't hesitate to use it even at the risk of mutual eradication. That's because their misguided faith teaches the glorification of dying and going to heaven to obtain unimaginable reward for destroying infidels in mortality. That type of faith certainly shows the downside for the dire circumstances we could find ourselves in if a scenario like that ever comes to fruition.

Well, enough of the downside even though there is more. Looking on the bright side of fervent faith is that it often enriches the circumstances of life for those who commit to it.

The lives of the faithful are routinely enhanced by committing to the doctrine of a post mortal heavenly existence if they live a moral and Christ-like existence. A firm belief in landing up in Hell guides them from engaging otherwise. Such morality benefits the positive quality of their circumstances in life. Of course, not all those who claim fervent faith end up living moral lives, but a significant percentage of them do.

Then there are those who have lost all hope in ever enjoying any degree of fruitful earthly existence. For example, the criminal who has been sentenced to confinement for the rest of whatever life remains. Repenting and engaging in a faith that promises a glorious post mortal eternal existence offers new hope and a way to alleviate the miserable circumstances of remaining despair. After all, the short number of years in mortality compared to eternity is miniscule and now much more easily navigated. The future is once again bright instead of unbearable.

I've become a believer in the power of positive thinking. For example, if a fervent religious believer is convinced a problem encountered can be solved by an extra- terrestrial being through the power of prayer, I think it's possible the power of positive thinking can help make it happen. Not from the help of a godly being, but it's still a positive result of faith if it works.

Fellowship among those who share the same faith is a definite positive. Meeting and planning together promote lifelong friendships providing the constructive benefits arising from a shared commitment to support and watch over each other. Religiously sponsored family activities can promote a positive outcome spurred on by a shared faith.

The positive aspects of harmless faith appear to improve the circumstances surrounding the lives of those who believe regardless of being founded on truth and reason. The worst outcomes most often arise with corrupt charlatans imposing toxic faith on those who are mentally/ emotionally unstable and thus especially vulnerable to charismatic mental manipulation.

FIVE

LAW AND ORDER

Law and order play a huge role in the circumstance humans find themselves navigating. In America, the creating, enforcing and judging of law are coordinated among three coequal branches of government at both the federal and state level. The legislative branch makes the law, the executive enforces it and the judicial determines guilt/ innocent and sentencing if warranted.

Worldwide, the systems of law and order differ significantly. In countries like North Korea, for example, the law is determined by a tyrannical dictator. Those living under the rule of such a despot have no say of what is legal and what's not. Disobeying the rules established by an autocratic ruler ends up with the offender spending most or all the rest of his/her life in a concentration camp or something similar. The circumstances of those living under these abhorrent conditions can result in a life hardly worth inhabiting. Personal freedom is essentially unobtainable

Other despotic led countries like Russia claim to exist more within the standard of a democratic society where the right to vote, for example, exists. That ends up being a sham where election results are commandeered by an autocrat like Putin while those protesting are severely threatened and even murdered. The roots of one's living circumstances under these conditions are negatively impaired resulting in an environment completely different than in America.

I was employed for 27 years as an FBI Special Agent stationed in California, Texas and Utah. This experience gave me great insight into the criminal justice system in America. I believed then the FBI represented the premier law enforcement institution in the world. One of the reasons was the effort to select the most qualified and honest candidates while offering a sufficiently high salary and generous retirement system to help discourage being corrupted by the criminal element. American's living circumstances benefit as a result.

Living conditions in other democratic countries can end up horrifying where law enforcement is tarnished. In Mexico, for instance, during the time I was serving, gangs involved in the drug trade compromised law enforcement to the extent citizens lived in fear with little confidence the police would intercede. The low pay of officers was no match for the bribes offered by the crooks. The result was the beneficial human circumstances created by honest policing was severely shattered.

Although living in America with its system of justice being about as good as it gets, it's far from perfect and it doesn't take long to point out some of its warts. For one thing, although rare, it's not absolutely impervious to corruption. That bit of illegality on the part of law enforcement can have a huge impact on the circumstances involving the lives of those adversely impacted.

During my employment with the FBI in Texas, I investigated two sheriffs who were subsequently convicted of taking bribes from members of organized crime. Citizens who had knowledge of the illegality on the part of those paying the bribes were in constant fear of becoming witnesses because it was common knowledge the sheriffs would find out and make their lives miserable. Living under such circumstances was a constant nightmare. I couldn't believe the outpouring of support I got for my part in putting one of the worst offenders behind bars resulting in an honest and respected replacement. It was like an enormous black cloud was suddenly lifted from the county at large.

I suspected and many others agreed one of the problems with sheriffs in Texas was they were elected instead of appointed. They often ran on a reduced tax burden including their own salary. The problem is they became beholden to the crooks who helped finance their elections. They knew their meagre incomes would more than be made up for by the bribes they received. Many were totally corrupted from the get-go.

Even when corruption isn't factored in, the quality of policing is negatively impacted when those enforcing the law are consumed with despicable personal characteristics like racism, Slipshod recruiting, poor training and simple incompetence on the job can prove devastating.

No matter America's positive reputation, determining innocence or guilt in our criminal justice system depends on the quality of the parts. The main parts include judges, prosecutors, defense attorneys and juries.

I never ran across a judge I thought was corrupt, but one in particular had it out for any cases before him investigated by the FBI. His rulings always seemed to favor the defense. Finding out he was going to be the judge on a case worked by the FBI was disheartening to say the least. The only instance I lost a case I should have won was with a federal judge who always seemed to favor the defense. The reality is judges are human with some ruling in accordance with some misguided prejudices. The negative circumstances in those instances can unfairly influence both defendants and victims.

A drug case I worked involved a corrupt defense attorney who represented all the targets I was investigating. That made it difficult to turn once against the other because he wouldn't allow that to happen. Luckily, we caught him with a stash of drugs in his barn and we got the judge to disqualify him from representing any of the defendants who almost immediately started turning on each other trying to get a better deal.

One sad fact in our criminal justice system is the quality of a defense attorney is directly proportional to a defendant's financial capability. Those able to afford a wizard of a defense attorney can mean the difference between a juries' finding of guilt or innocence. It's been proven numerous times an innocent defendant ended up in prison or worse due to inadequate counsel.

The competence and tenacity of a prosecutor can also make a huge difference in the lives of all involved. Just like defense attorneys, a superior qualified prosecutor can make the difference in convincing a jury thus preventing a guilty party from going free. On the other hand, an incompetent one can result in the opposite.

I've run across prosecutors who should have pursued another occupation because of their timid reluctance to function at trial. Often the result was a guilty defendant receiving less of a punishment than deserved because the prosecutor offered a minimalist plea agreement just to prevent the pressure of facing a jury.

Finally, and of no small import, you never know about how a jury will rule. Even if they haven't been threatened or bribed by a defendant, they can be swayed by both prosecutor and defense attorney from reaching a just verdict. No matter the effort to impanel an impartial pool, the members are subject to human frailty and many times the resulting verdict ends up being the luck of the draw.

Anyone who claims America represents equal justice for all doesn't know what they're talking about. Even so, it's arguably a system superior to the rest of the world and something we can be proud of and continue striving to improve. The circumstances surrounding the lives of all those impacted depend on it.

SIX

INTELLIGENCE

Intelligence is a significant root cause of the positive and negative living circumstances humans find themselves inhabiting. In general, those with superior brain power have a better chance of succeeding in life than those who aren't so fortunate. That doesn't mean other factors can't mitigate the difference, but everything else equal, superior intellect provides a huge advantage for those fortunate to have received such exceptional mental related DNA at birth.

I'm not an expert on the best way to measure mental acuity. I'll accede to the measure of one's intelligent quotient (IQ) as the method I'm personally familiar with. There's likely wiggle room in the results depending on the conditions under which such tests are administered.

An IQ of from 90-110 signifies average intelligence covering just above 50 % of the population. A score of between 111-120 is deemed above average and applies to about 16%. Gifted is 121-130 for about 6.5% and very gifted greater than 130 for about 2%.

For those below average, a score of 80-90 applies to just under 16% and 70-90 is identified as cognitively impaired applying to about 6.4% of the population.

I think I may have had an IQ test, but I'm not sure. My best guess now is I probably follow somewhere in the average category not bad enough to be lower, but likely not much higher either. That's because I've never been smart when it came to schooling getting by more on persistence than brain power to get slightly above average grades.

I compare myself to a good friend who is highly intelligent. We went through Officer Candidate School together. The course required academic performance. He listened to lectures once and passed exams with flying colors with little or no further study. Myself, on the other hand, had to go over and over the course material to just barely pass by the skin of my teeth.

The same thing with the University of Utah where we both graduated with a degree in accounting. The difference was he had a full-time job and got high grades just by absorbing the lectures by teachers without even needing to buy text books. For every hour of study on his part, I'm sure I spend 10 times as long to get by. I'm sure he has a photographic memory. If his IQ is less than 130, I'd be surprised.

Although we somehow ended up pretty much equal in achievement when looking back in our retirement, I'm confident the only reason was my concerted persistence to match his accomplishment with considerably less effort. Otherwise, the circumstance of his life would have ended up much more successful than mine. As is, his was a much easier life experience to negotiate.

A high IQ more often than not is buoyed by a superior lifestyle with all the extra perks that accompany it. Those with low IQs are frequently not so fortunate resulting in numerous struggles not encountered by those higher up the IQ scale.

One measure of the benefit of a higher IQ relates to the ability to more successfully navigate the educational ladder. According to the U.S. Census Bureau, 88% of America graduated high school or earned a GED in 2015. 55% earned a bachelor's degree or higher. Amelia Josephson, a writer well known for analyzing financial topics, published a study concerning the earning potential for those mentally capable of negotiating higher levels of educational achievement.

The report at the time of her research in 2015 indicated the average initial salary for those with less than a high school diploma was $25,636/year. For those graduating high school, the average was $35, 256/ yr. For those with some college but no degree, it was $38,376/yr. Those with an associate degree earned $41,496/ yr. while those with a bachelor's degree earned $59,124. A master's degree garnered a yearly salary of $69,732. Those with degrees higher than that continued with the same upward trend.

It doesn't mean there aren't exceptions to the norm. There are instances when someone doesn't graduate high school and ends up a millionaire. Just like someone with an IQ of 130 somehow screws up and ends up a pauper. Nevertheless, the chances are considerably more likely of someone with a high IQ leading a more fulfilling life than someone with a low one

Intelligence makes a difference. The life situation of those benefitting from superior brain power is more often than not rewarded with a secure and rewarding lifestyle more difficult to achieve by those not so fortunate.

SEVEN

PHYSICAL HEALTH

Human health is at the root of the positive/negative circumstances encountered during our sojourn in mortality. Health applies to both physical and mental. I'll concentrate on physical in this chapter and leave mental to the next.

I've experienced on a couple of occasions a hellish nightmare temporarily dominating my life when my normally good health and pleasant lifestyle took steep nose dives. The first was catching whooping cough in my 60s. For over a year thereafter, I experienced a tortured existence. Everything that gave me joy had to be put on hold. For the first 4 months, a gut-wrenching cough dominating every hour of the day cutting my ability to sleep to just 2-3 hours every night. What followed was a horrible bout of asthma making it difficult to walk to the mail box and back and requiring the use of an oxygen tank to restore my breathing.

Finally recovered and back to normal for the next 10 years, I all of a sudden caught a rare malady called Guillain Barre Syndrome

(GBS). Once again, for the next year, my life circumstances were pretty much limited to suffering and trying to recover. The pain in my back was excruciating resulting in my inability to get a good night's sleep and requiring the constant ingestion of opiates with the side effect of agonizing constipation (too much information).

GBS caused my inability to walk. Apparently, renegade antibodies normally fighting a virus turned on my nerves stripping the coating and short circuiting the connection with my brain required to coordinate with my legs. It took me several months in a care facility devoted to physical therapy and a balance clinic to relearn how to walk starting with a wheel chair to a walker to a cane and finally once again on my own. Being in the care center was something I never again want to repeat. My theretofore pleasurable living circumstances were temporarily gutted.

The point is my experience was minimal when compared to the health tragedies encountered by billions of others. I lived a life consumed by constant misery for only a couple of my 77 years so far. The state of one's physical health can result in a life worth living or one not so much.

There are several causes of bad health. One of the worst with no human capability to prevent is inheriting bad DNA. For example, although there are other preventable environmental causes like cigarette smoke, becoming heir to defective cancer genes is unavoidable. The only response is to attempt a cure.

Negotiating various cure attempts, even if ultimately successful, can interrupt the quality of life for the duration of treatment. Never assured of a cure can consume every waking hour. The fear of premature death often ruins any chance of experiencing a satisfying life experience. Cancer is only one of the many dreaded inherited genes with similar awful outcomes.

Humans can be their own worst enemies when it comes to preventing illness having nothing to do to inherited susceptibility. The quality of one's living condition can run the gambit from excellent to poor depending on the effort or lack thereof to make a difference. Although no guarantee, the chances for avoiding troubling health concerns like diabetes and heart problems are improved by watching weight gain, eating healthy and exercising. Regular yearly checkups including blood tests etc. can help prevent one or more budding concerns before getting out of control.

The 2020 Covid-19 pandemic threatening the health and lives of millions around the world offers an example how potential victims have it in their control to determine the circumstances surrounding their lives. Precautions like social distancing, wearing masks, staying away from crowded venues and using sanitizer can help insure a positive although cautious lifestyle. Ignoring such vigilance is a personal decision that can result in a devastating outcome negatively altering any previously gratifying state of human existence.

A person's good or negative health is a major factor concerning the positive or negative circumstance of their personal state of human affairs. Some health concerns can't be avoided and others are within the human capability to minimize or eliminate adverse consequences

EIGHT

MENTAL HEALTH

The role of poor mental health and its adverse circumstantial effects on the lives of those suffering from it, including those closely associated, are often underestimated in my non-professional opinion. There are so many mental health defects out there, it's hard to estimate the total devastation caused as a result. I'll mention a small sample of the following more common categories:

Psychopathy is defined as "a mental disorder in which an individual manifests amoral and antisocial behavior, lack of ability to love or establish meaningful personal relationships, extreme egocentricity, failure to learn from experience," etc. That's likely to play a significant role in the quality of life on the part of victims and those closely related.

I can manage the sad situation surrounding a spouse, for example, who unknowingly weds someone who's a psychopath. They have one or more children before it becomes apparent living with someone incapable of love or establishing a meaningful relationship isn't worth sticking it out any longer. The resulting chaos can make life a living nightmare.

Bipolar disorder is another mental deficiency defining the quality of life for those involved. Formerly called manic depression, it is a mental health condition causing extreme mood swings that include emotional highs (mania or hypomania). The downside is depression, hopelessness and losing interest or pleasure in most daily activities.

Bipolar is a confounding mental impairment determining the human state of affairs. During an emotional high, life is regulated by a sense of wellbeing superior to the normal mind. On the other end, it's exactly opposite. What a way to go through life. It has to be an exhausting and overall terrifying condition to have to navigate. Certainly, nothing like the preferable living atmosphere of those not so inflicted.

Narcissism is a mental disorder with a broad spectrum of human defects. Eight common traits include: (1) Grandiosity, an unrealistic view of oneself believing they are more important than others. (2) Arrogant and domineering thinking they are superior to everyone else while attempting to control and dominate them. (3) Consumed with personal success and power. (4) Lack of empathy displaying an inability to care about the feelings and misfortune of others. (5) Belief of being unique with no one else coming close to being as important and superior. (6) Extreme sense of entitlement for anything they want and desire. (7) Requiring excessive admiration with no tolerance for anyone compromising their place in the spotlight. (8) Exploitive taking advantage of others for personal benefit unconcerned for the damage inflicted on those so compromised.

The life experience of a narcist is problematic for those suffering from the disorder due mostly to the inability to gain the trust and support of others because of their selfish self-absorption. That can end up minimizing their ability to be successful in both work and personal relationships.

Worse are the lives of those who are adversely affected due to being subjected to such a person for any number of reasons.

Schizophrenia is fairly common mental disorder with more than 3 million cases per year in the US. It's common for ages 18-35 and more common in males. Symptoms include delusion, hallucinations, agitation, disordered thinking, inappropriate reaction, phobia, and lack of pleasure.

Amazing to me was the mental disorder with the highest mortality rate is Anorexia Nervosa. The danger to those possessing this mental ailment include heart, kidney and liver failure; osteoporosis; anemia; electrolyte imbalance; low blood sugar; gastrointestinal failure; amenorrhea: fertility failure and suicide. The tragic living circumstances for anyone suffering through this vicious eating disorder is obvious. The lives of those who love and care for those afflicted can end up tragically.

This has been a short list of many more mental disorders, but I think enough to make the point the lives of those who suffer from or care about those suffering can be significantly impacted in ways that distract from the ability to live a productive and enjoyable existence.

Luckily, mental illness can be successfully treated for many victims through professional therapists and a wide range of mental altering drugs. One problem, for example for those suffering from bipolar disorder, is refusing the medication because the drug not only helps heal the low state, but prevents the high euphoria. They are simply not willing to eliminate the ecstasy stage. Maintaining the regular and constant ingestion of curative drugs for all mental impairments is paramount to regaining a more normal living experience.

NINE

PHYSICAL APPEAL

Handsome and gorgeous refer to the lucky humans who were born with attractive producing DNA giving them a huge circumstantial advantage in living the kind of unrivaled life experience the rest of us can only hope to at least partially duplicate.

Rationalizing beauty is in the eye of the beholder, the stark reality is it's much more significant than that. That doesn't mean someone with stupendous physical features can't downgrade their advantage by messing up in other ways. Nevertheless, such fortunate humans begin life's journey more likely to succeed.

Personally, I would have loved to have been born a babe magnet. Not even close even though I wasn't totally ugly. All the way through school, the cute girls were attracted to the guys with an attractive mug and a muscled torso. To be honest, I wasn't attracted to the girls whose faces and bodies were less than appealing.

Eventually, I was somewhat shocked when my attractive future spouse agreed to my marriage proposal. What was she thinking? Probably a mistake to turn down her dad's offer of a new car if she dumped me. Too late now after 55 years of matrimonial bliss, at least on my part.

I recall one particular experience when I was working a case as an FBI Special Agent and assigned to work with an Assistant US Attorney who was a hunk as the girls would say. He was pretty much a duplicate of John Kennedy Jr. It astounded me how one good-looking girl after another made passes to get his attention. I never had one that ever made a pass to me. It was an amazing experience to witness first- hand time after time the advantage superlative DNA can provide.

It's not really fair when you think about it; especially, for those who turn out truly unattractive through no fault of their own. Going through life with that kind of continual disadvantage has to be difficult and often heartbreaking. Realizing that others don't perceive you in a favorable light has to hurt even if you learn to live somewhat normally since that's the only option that makes any sense. "Why me?" has to be in the back of one's mind when trying to justify the unfairness of it all.

The chance of being a successful movie star, model, TV personality etc. is much more easily obtained by the babe and guy magnets. Those not so endowed can achieve similar success but it's nowhere near as easy. My wife has a framed picture of Robert Redford at his prime on the wall. Not that I blame her, but a photo of me hasn't made it past the confines of a photo album.

I've got no room to complain. I went to high school in Wiesbaden, Germany with Pricilla Presley when her last name was still Beaulieu. I played saxophone in a rock band. She was by far the most gorgeous girl in school. It wasn't even close. At a dance we were performing at, I made an unsuccessful attempt at impressing her and ask her to dance. She was polite but was more interested in dating Elvis which I could never understand.

Later with 5 grown teenage daughters, they didn't believe my claim involving Pricilla. I wrote her a letter and she responded with a nice photo autographed with some very complimentary comments included. She hadn't forgotten me. You guessed it. A framed picture has since adorned the wall.

Good looking men and women attract each other and that mutual attraction can benefit offspring for untold generations to follow. Others not so attractive mate with those similarly endowed resulting in the lives of countless offspring unable to enjoy the same built-in advantages of those born attractive.

Of course, handsome men and gorgeous women can reduce their advantage by failing to maintain their edge. One example we've all noticed are spectacular-looking men and women gaining excessive weight magically transforming into nothing recognizable from their previous exceptional physical persona. A deplorable personality can also negate any advantage What a waste nullifying such a fortunate DNA benefit.

Plastic surgery, surgical fat removal and breast augmentation have played a role in the intense desire to become more attractive or maintain attractiveness while growing older. Ill-conceived surgery gone awry can make life miserable as a tragic aftereffect. In many cases, those who were born genetically attractive make things worse when they would have maintained a better appearance by letting nature take its course with a little help from non-evasive makeup.

Those less handsome and gorgeous can increase their chance of approaching the benefits so easily achieved by the attractive crowd by how they act and treat others. Sometime that results in favoring the less enticing due a great personality, sense of humor and a selfless caring attitude. Beauty often loses its inbred appeal by someone who acts like a jerk.

However, all things considered, the difference of being born attractive and not so much results in providing a significant advantage to the former. Physical appeal is an undeniable root cause in the diverse living circumstances humans find themselves negotiating.

TEN

EMPLOYMENT

The circumstances humans end up living under are undoubtedly affected by issues of employment. A job not only influences the state of affairs of the employee but the lives of those dependent on the worker.

Employment is essential to provide a reasonable standard of living. That standard can run the gamut from just barely getting by or worse to living a life of opulence and all that goes with it. It's hard to argue against the obvious that the quality of life is generally superior under conditions of the latter rather than the former. Of course, there are always exceptions to the obvious where life can end up more pleasant for those of minimal means than the super-rich. But it's hard to deny that not needing to worry about putting food on the table leads to a less stressful lifestyle.

It's my opinion landing a well-paying and satisfying job dates back to high school. Students who take their education seriously and do their best to get good grades are well ahead of those who don't in the ultimate hunt to be selected for quality occupational opportunities. Why is it some do and some don't feel that urgency?

What part do students on their own, parents, and teachers play in creating the desire to excel as early as high school. The obvious answer is all three are critical. Some students are born with the trait of surpassing the norm not matter what other disincentives might be present. Some will rebel against parents and purposely neglect studies just to spite them. Others are more submissive and will achieve good grades just to please their parents.

Excellent teachers can make a huge difference and bad ones can have the opposite effect. We've all experienced the former and remember how we enjoyed attending class and how our desire to learn more was positively influenced. On the other hand, I recall some really unqualified teachers that bored me to death and I may have considered dropping out altogether had all my instructors proved that deficient.

Decent paying jobs do exist for those not going on to college. As discussed previously, a lower IQ may prevent excelling therein. There are certain trades that can prove fairly lucrative but the chances of similar success in comparison to obtaining a higher degree are less likely. Statistics prove that to be the case.

According to a 2019 study by the U.S. Bureau of Statistics, the median weekly earnings for persons age 25 and over was as follows:

Master's degree	$3,248
Bachelor's degree	$1,248
Associate's degree	$887
Lesser college	$833
High School degree	$746
No high school degree	$592

Of course, those achieving advanced degrees to become doctors, dentists, and other high paying professions can earn explosive incomes off the chart.

Job satisfaction plays an integral part in the enjoyment of life. Being tethered to a job solely out of necessity to pay the bills can be a major drag if that's the only benefit. The sooner a student can pinpoint the kind of work he would prefer based on personnel gratification, the better.

From the day I entered college, I knew I wanted to work for the US government. A primary reason was how much my dad enjoyed his job as a civilian with the US Air Force. It offered him the opportunity to travel to Morocco, Germany and Bermuda at taxpayer expense. There was no fear of losing his job unless he did something illegal or stupid. A generous retirement was pretty much guaranteed, unlike private employment where benefits can be yanked at the last moment.

That early determination on my part resulted in a thoroughly enjoyable 34 career with the Air Force, the Department of Interior and the FBI. Not only resulting in financial benefits above the norm, I actually looked forward most mornings to heading out to the office to see what new gratifying challenges were bound to unfold.

Low paying and despised employment bleads over to lack of contentment in family life. Spousal arguments are often tied to money concerns and worker discontent carrying over to strained relationships sometimes resulting to physical and emotional abuse. Poor relationships between parents carry over to children; especially, when divorce is the ultimate outcome.

Although it might not seem fair to place such a burden on those of high school age, the best chance of achieving a productive and enjoyable life is to start working toward achieving a rewarding employment opportunity at this early age. It might mean forgoing some temporary gratification but will in the long run prove well worth the sacrifice and effort. Life normally lasts a lot longer than adolescence.

ELEVEN

ADDICTION

Addiction plays a huge role surrounding the circumstantial quality of life for those suffering from its insidious complications. Addiction takes many forms including smoking, illegal drug use, alcoholism, pornography, gambling, and slew of other similar ruinous mental and physical dependences. I'll just touch on a few of them noting that my comments most likely reflect similarly on the rest.

Alcoholism is an addiction that appears to have a genetic/hereditary component. That doesn't mean other unrelated factors can't play a role, but genetics may be a prime factor fueling the destructive result.

One estimate suggests that as many as 18 million adults in American struggle with alcohol use disorder; that's one in 12 adults. Around 100,000 people die every year including deaths due to cirrhosis of the liver and other organ damage. It also increases the risk of kidney disease, diabetes, and several cancers. It's a significant root cause resulting in a serious impediment for countless sufferers severely constrained from leading a productive lifestyle.

I'm confident I don't have what it takes to be alcohol addicted. I had sufficient opportunity in my college days as a member of Sigma Phi Epsilon to succumb if all it took was drinking too much over an extended period of time. The thought of needing a drink early in the day, one of the indications of becoming alcoholic, never crossed my mind. In fact, the thought of such turned my stomach.

Family, twin, and adoption studies have shown that alcoholism definitely has a genetic component. In 1990, Blum et al. proposed an association between the A1 allele of the DRD2 gene and alcoholism. The DRD2 gene was the first candidate gene that showed promise of an association with alcoholism.

Alcohol in moderation for those not genetically vulnerable can actually enhance quality livability. Jill Weisenberger, MS, RDN, CDE, a dietitian nutritionist and author in Newport News, VA. says, "Consuming alcohol in moderation is associate with reduced risk of Type 2 diabetes and less risk of dying from heart disease while protecting the heart by increasing HDL cholesterol" –the good kind. Additionally, the phytonutrients and other antioxidant compounds in red wine may further benefit the heart by protecting blood vessels from oxidative damage.

The quandary is deciding whether the health benefit is worth the risk of addiction. It's better never to take the first drink if there has been a family history of alcoholism. Even if there is none, a wise course of action is to make a determined effort toward moderation. A DWI rap sheet can have a devastating effect on benefitting from what a non-criminal record has to offer.

Unlike a glass of red wine in the evening, there's no upside to nicotine addiction from smoking. It's all bad and no good. The risks with a smoking habit are no longer debatable. Luckily for me, my first experience with taking a puff occurred when I was about 7 years old. My negligent teenage babysitter let me try. I coughed and choked. It was horrible. I have never had any kind of urge to try it again.

Unfortunately, peer pressure among teenagers can coerce continued experimentation until inhaling and exhaling is mastered and nicotine takes a firm hold. Trying to break the routine thereafter can evolve into a lifelong and miserable struggle. Simply acknowledging the health risk is too often insufficient to break the habit.

Lung cancer isn't the only malady caused by smoking. Chronic bronchitis, serious asthma and obstructive pulmonary disease often result. Coronary heart disease including heart attack aneurysm, stroke and vascular disease add to a long list of preventable and life-threatening ailments.

Vaping (E-cigarettes) became a craze by teens under the false assumption by some as being a safer alternative to tobacco. Not true. Research showed it also increased the risk of respiratory disease and has been linked to lung cancer. Also, harmful to cardiovascular health, increased blood pressure and interfering with healthy brain function. Nicotine is once again the addictive curse.

As an FBI Special Agent, I was case agent investigating illegal drug cases in Texas. One in particular involved a major amphetamine ring including numerous victims addicted to this all-consuming villainous concoction. I was a personal witness to the devastating drama ruining any chance of addicted users realizing a life worth living.

Amphetamine addicts stay up for days with no sleep and then crash for long periods when their bodies can no longer take the pressure. This destructive cycle can turn otherwise healthy young adults into exactly the opposite. Heroin and cocaine use are just as insidious in ruining a life, not to mention ending up in prison and minimizing the chance of achieving decent employment even after released from incarceration.

Excessive legal opioid consumption is just as bad affecting law-abiding citizens deceived by the pharmaceutical industry and negligent physicians as a safe course in treating severe pain. Once hooked, the damaging effect on the quality of life is not easily distinguishable from the devastation encountered by the intake of illegal drugs.

There's no doubt addiction in whatever form is a primary root in fomenting the negative circumstances of a pathetic although mostly preventable life experience.

TWELVE

GOVERNMENT

Government plays a major role in the lives of humans who find the circumstances of their existence impacted for both good and bad by those in charge. Chapter 5 already discussed the part played by law and order. This chapter will analyze what else affects the daily lives of billions finding themselves subject to a wide range of governmental régimes.

The worst are those where authoritative dictators have wormed their way into power and the public can either conform to their selfish dictates or pay the price which too often results in unlawful confinement or even premature death. Having little freedom or say-so in one's life is similar to being jailed without the bars. Being subjugated to a tyrannical autocrat like Kim Jong-un in North Korea has to be traumatic living in constant fear of doing something to draw his psychopathic ire.

Living in alleged democratic Russia under Putin is somewhat better, but the same kind of fear is ever-present. Running against him in a sham election is paramount to asking for a date with your favorite cemetery. Ask the latest victim, Russian opposition leader Alexei Navalny poisoned with polonium 210 narrowly escaping instant death unlike a half dozen other previous critics of the Putin regime.

Russia and North Korea obviously aren't alone in the world of corrupt autocrats wickedly controlling the lives of citizens while selfishly living in the glow of extreme opulence afforded by their ruthless rule. Saudi Arabia, Venezuela, and China are just a few more of the governments that immediately come to mind, but there are dozens more restricting the rights of citizens to conduct their lives free from constant fear and unconscionable subjugation.

I'll spend the rest of the chapter on America similar to other democracies around the world. Although far superior to living under a corrupt dictatorship, lives can still be significantly impacted for good or bad depending on which political party controls federal and state government.

The lives of Americans are significantly affected by the action of legislators voted into office. We haven't always been a country with equal opportunity for all. Blacks have spent a lot of the past 244 years subjected to all the disadvantages extreme racism promotes. Women have been similarly marginalized preventing their right to vote until August 18, 1920 when the 19th amendment of the U.S. Constitution was finally ratified.

Admittedly being a progressive Democrat, I contend the offices of President of the United States and Governors of the 50 states have a huge impact on the circumstantial living conditions of those living under their leadership. That couldn't be any clearer evaluating President Trump's term in office. My belief is that if he had gotten another 4 years, American democracy would have suffered exponentially and ended up a 2nd rate nation. With Biden, I think we have a chance to recover all we've forfeited during Trump's first term.

A few of the significant legislative topics that will make a difference in the lives of all of us and our posterity include climate change, health care, immigration, gun control, infrastructure, taxing, policing, voter suppression and white supremist terrorist organizations. Trump and Biden were and still do represent opposite sides of all these issues. Depending on the integrity of the makeup of Congress, the quality of life in America could be vastly improved or damaged beyond repair for years to come.

The same goes for the governors and legislators of state government. A similar peril rears its ugly head if failing to positively address the above stated critical issues.

Ultimately, free and fair elections in democracies at both the local and federal level provide the required root strength for improving the circumstantial living conditions for all involved. Voting out those leaders representing the worst of potential outcomes is critical regardless of party affiliation. Otherwise, voters deserve what they get.

THIRTEEN

WEALTH

Wealth can make a huge difference in the lifestyle between the wealthy and those of more modest means. The number of different ways in which wealth is accumulated or lost is substantial. Whatever those ways may be and the resulting consequences, the lasting effect can result in a life worth living vs.one less appealing.

Those well-healed aren't necessarily more content than those barely making ends meet. Extreme depression, for example, can negate the advantages of affluence. But everything else being equal, it's hard to argue that having no money worries minimizes the concerns that otherwise attach to a lower standard of living.

Prior to the 2020 pandemic, my wife and I enjoyed taking a break from the winter cold in Utah to Newport Beach in California. It amazed us to observe the huge volume of luxury cars and multi-million-dollar homes gracing the cliffs overlooking the Pacific. How did so many accumulate that much wealth. We guessed they must be involved in the lucrative movie industry or they inherited enormous wealth from their parents or other wealthy relatives. If true, that helps explain just a couple of the limitless causes of how human living conditions diverge.

The quality of vacations varies depending on the amount of money you can afford to spend. At 6'4", I can personally testify how much more pleasant a vacation to Europe was when I finally was able to afford round-trip tickets in first class. The same goes for the quality of hotels and the ability to afford first-class excursions. I beg to argue with anyone claiming the amount of available money to spend doesn't affect the consequential enjoyment of a holiday experience.

Unfortunately, America's current tax system has rewarded the rich over those not so favorably endowed. It appears at the end of 2020; it was President Trump and his Republican supporters in congress who succumbed to rich donors thus exasperating that unfair advantage. The sad fact is the complicated tax code concocted to favor the wealthy has resulted in many of the richest corporations paying little or no tax. The argument of trickle-down economics has been proven totally spurious to say the least.

The 2017 tax reduction act promoted by Trump primarily rewarded the super-rich who needed a tax break the least. The tax for well-off corporations was significantly lowered thus reducing a critical source to fund the government. The national deficit soared. Lowering personal tax rates similarly significantly favored the richest 1% of taxpayers who least needed a financial boost. Those of lower means who could have used a tax break the most received only a trifling token benefit.

Raising 5 daughters meant that some months I had to pay the minimum on my credit card debt to meet my other monthly expenses that didn't allow for deferred payment. But that was about the worst it got. The circumstances of my life weren't negatively altered because of my moderate level of wealth. I can't imagine the worrisome and even terrifying state of affairs for those less fortunate struggling to financially stay afloat.

I can only try to envision losing sleep, loss of appetite, family squabbles, depression, and many other troubling dents in a happy lifestyle arising from the worry associated with insufficient wealth to smooth things out. Going to the extreme like suffering through non-existent health insurance, bankruptcy or losing a house to repossession would significantly lessen the joy in life that might otherwise have been possible.

The accumulation of wealth varies from easy-peasy for some to a concerted struggle for others. Those that inherit excessive wealth may have problems adjusting to a satisfactory lifestyle in other ways, but having more than sufficient money to eliminate the concerns of being poor is essentially a non-issue.

For those of us not so fortunate, we have to depend on our own fortitude and ingenuity to accumulate what we need to reduce the financial pressures that have the capability of inducing excessive stress and desperation.

As previously mentioned, some impediments like low IQ and debilitating physical/mental health make achieving financial stability a lot harder. But for most of us not so burdened, it comes down to personal responsibility and the perseverance to improve our station in life. We kind of make our own beds and will ultimately have to live with the result of how well we have met the challenge.

FOURTEEN

LOCATION

As savvy relators proclaim "LOCATION- LOCATION" as being the most important element in ensuring the rising value of a home, that same slogan applies to the circumstance humans face depending on where they end up living.

I've lived in 11 different locations during by 77 years on earth, and each one involved a unique set of living conditions. It made a difference in what the environments at the time determined I was faced with. I've spent time in 6 different foreign countries noting a similar diversity in what living there had to offer.

Without covering all 11 locations and 6 foreign countries, I'll make the point by sharing just a few personal examples involving the varied circumstances encountered from living in different locations; those differences being significant root causes for how my life experience turned out.

As a teenager, I lived for two years on a fenced-in airbase in Morocco where my dad was employed with the Airforce. That experience resulted in a totally different environment had I attended high school back in Utah. My fellow students were only there for a few years and thus the relationships were temporary with little ability to form exclusionary cliques like formed stateside. The student body was far more racially diverse than in Utah. I feel that improved by ability to quickly form positive human connections.

My best friend in Morocco ended up living in England to this very day. We keep in regular touch and I've been able to visit him and get a reading on what it's like to live there. One of the primary differences is his National Health Insurance coverage never needing to concern himself with deductibles, co-pays, or any contentious dealings with private health insurance companies. He goes to a doctor just down the street from where he lives with his only concern being treatment Any ailment of a serious nature is immediately addressed.

There can be a reasonable debate on the pros and cons, but there was no doubt at the feeling of calm felt by my friend involving any health concerns which is anything but common involving those living under the privatized system employed in America. After retirement, he didn't have to pay taxes for coverage. Ask those unfortunates in America who find themselves taking bankruptcy when a health disaster they couldn't avoid ruined their previously secure standard of living.

As newlyweds, we lived for two years just off Fisherman's Wharf in San Francisco with a population of almost 900 thousand and then two years in Kanab Utah populated by just under 5 thousand. Obviously, the different circumstances living in the two environments were huge. It wasn't a matter of which location was preferable. Each ended up with experiences superior to the other. Each had its deficiencies.

One of the most enjoyable experiences in our young married life was living in San Francisco; experiences not possible had we remained in Utah. The Golden Gate Bridge, the Redwoods, the Bay, the fog, the cable cars etc. etc. made our life a living dream. Unfortunately, that dream couldn't continue if we wanted to raise a family which we wanted to do. It was just too expensive to transfer from our small apartment to a house. We just made ends meet including both our salaries.

My wife cried for weeks after transferring to Kanab due to a dearth of acceptable housing even though being far more affordable. She cried two years later because we hated to move away. We had some of the best times in our lives living in red-rock country close to the North Rim of the Grand Canyon and countless fun destinations within short drives with our purchase of a 4-wheel Jeep. We hauled our garbage to the dump. Nobody locked their houses or cars. Everybody waved when passing by in our cars. Life was hard to beat.

The problem with Kanab was my job which ended up boring me to death. Also, the unlikely prospect of improving my financial lot in life. That would require becoming an FBI Special Agent and moving once again to large metropolitan areas including Los Angeles and Dallas with all the lifestyle changes that would once again entail.

The point is where you end up living for whatever reason will impact the circumstances you find yourself encountering. Those outcomes will vary all the way from unsatisfying to terrific.

FIFTEEN

MOTHER NATURE

Mother Nature controls all our lives. Temperature, rain, wind, and storms compose the main components controlling the circumstances of our daily living agenda. These forces of nature can both bless and curse us. Blessings include the right amount of heat to keep our bodies from freezing without constantly relying on fire. Moisture and heat from the sun help produce the water and food our bodies require to survive.

This chapter will deal primarily with one of the worst curses known as climate change. The number of humans adversely affected continues to rise and ultimately could result in annihilation of a significant portion of humanity unless controlled.

The setback related to climate change occurs when the temperature on the earth rises due to greenhouse gases trapping more heat in the atmosphere. With the result being increasing global surface temperatures, droughts and more intense storms unfolding. That then can produce catastrophic fire and flood events. Observing the disastrous fires in

California in 2020 portends only the tip of a dire future unless corrective measures are immediately instituted.

While increased storm rain in some areas might provide plenty of drinking water, the increased warming and reduced snowpack in other dry mountainous areas depending on Spring runoff may have the exact opposite effect. The continuing rise in temperature in states like Arizona could make such locations miserable to inhabit.

The dire predictions of climate scientists are happening sooner than initially predicted. Proof is the accelerated melting of the massive glaciers at the poles. That increases oceanic levels that could wipe out major population centers around the world. Can you even begin to imagine the massive altering of your circumstantial living conditions if you lived there? Your life would pretty much turn into one of those featured disaster movies we deem highly unlikely. Maybe not so implausible after all.

Although including chlorofluorocarbons, nitrous oxide and methane, the primary culprit in clogging the atmosphere is the increase in carbon dioxide caused by human activities like deforestation (trees absorb CO_2), land use changes, but primarily by the burning of fossil fuels like oil.

The obvious solution to positively impact the future of all humans is to ditch fossil fuels as soon as humanly possible and replace the need for power with clean energy supplied by solar, wind and even the possibility of nuclear power.

The problem during President Trump's term in office was he has minimized the threat of global warming while encouraging the expansion of fossil fuel production. He ridiculed the idea of transforming into clean energy. The fact he willingly succumbed to the pressure of big oil and its attempt to corner the energy market is significant to say the least. He falsely claimed curtailing the production of fossil fuels would lead to a massive loss of jobs.

The reality is more likely the opposite, Not only working to reduce global warming, converting to clean energy would mean adding more well-paying jobs than those lost. Regardless, there's no comparison to the loss of jobs if unrestricted climate change exacts it's predicted toll. It's hard to live a life worth living if you lose your home by fire or flood and can't feed your family because climate change has turned your life upside down.

In my conversations with climate change deniers, it's often argued that even if it's true, any real damage is far in the future. I respond that sounds a little selfish to me. I ask them why it is they apparently aren't concerned about their children and their children down the line. Sometimes that stops them in their tracks for a moment, but then they return to the claim the whole theory of climate change is a theoretical hoax. Oh, well!

Recently, a study by a team from Michigan Technological University confirmed that 97% of scientists agree climate change is caused by humans. The study was compiled from an analysis of seven previous independent studies qualifying it as a mega-study. It "found that the more knowledge of climate science these scientists have, the more likely they are to believe in human-caused change."

That being true, it means humans, if they respond quickly, have the capability to stop relying on fossil fuels to power their lives; thus, dramatically improving their chance and that of their posterity to live lives worth living.

Honestly, I'm a bit pessimistic because there appears little urgency by most of those with whom I share my concern. You would think that lack of awareness to the potential global disaster would flood the news. You would think that lack of alarm would be dispelled by the current plight of the thousands of ruined lives due to massive fires and multiple hurricanes in California and the Gulf Coast. Apparently, it going to have to get even worse to garner the attention such carnage deserves.

Yes, mother nature has played and will undoubtedly play an even greater future role in the weather- related catastrophes humans face while struggling through an ever-worsening climate-warming bottleneck.

SIXTEEN

GENDER

Depending on the chromosome one has been awarded at birth, that's a significant factor dictating the circumstances humans find themselves facing. If the fetus draws the XX chromosome, a female is born and if XY, a male. It's kind of the luck of the draw.

Gender inequality is a topic written about seemingly without end so I won't try to cover all the aspects most of us are already familiar with hearing about. Instead, I'll mention a few of the more prominent inequities to emphasis how something as small as a chromosome can have such an enormous impact on a life experience.

Arguably, one of the greatest inequalities plaguing women concerns the Islamic religion forcing the acceptance that men are superior to women. There's the one-half rule stating, for example, a women's testimony is equal to only half that of a man and, in any inheritance, the women's share is worth only half the amount awarded to a man. Males are in charge and women must accept that supremacy as the will of Allah who has predestined them to live as submissive, obedient wives.

Forget the pride of having an attractive figure and face. The Muslim women must pay special attention to the clothes they wear. Clothing must be loosely fitted making sure no cleavage is revealed. Normally, they choose to wear an abaya to help hide any curvature. A hijab is required to be worn in much of the far-east to hide a women's face. For example, in the Indonesian Aceh province, Muslim women are required to wear one as are all women in Iran.

Women in America have fared better, but it hasn't been a bowl of cherries. America's early history is replete with women being denied some of the basic rights enjoyed by men. Married women once couldn't own property and had no legal claim to any money they might earn. No female had the right to vote. Women were supposed to focus on housework and motherhood while refraining from any political activity.

It took until August 26, 1920 for the 19th Amendment to be certified by U.S. Secretary of State Bainbridge Colby. Women finally achieved the right to vote throughout the United States. Eight million women voted in elections for the first time that year. Even so, it took over 60 years for the remaining 12 states to ratify the 19th Amendment. Mississippi was the last to do so, on March 22, 1984.

Employment inequities have continued to plague the rights of women to the present day. Studies have revealed the following statistics: (1) only 4.8 % of Fortune 500 CEOs are women. (2) Only 40% of management positions are held by females. (3) Those doing the hiring are 13% more likely to click on the application of a male candidate. (4) Women on average are 30% less likely to be called for a job interview, (5) When men are doing the hiring, there's only a 40% chance of a women being selected; when women do the hiring, that rises to 50%.

Depending on ethnicity, women earn less than men for the same jobs. African women earn just 62.5 cents on the dollar while Hispanic women earn just 54.4 cents. White women earn about 79 cents per dollar compared with white men.

The women's "Me Too" movement has finally brought more attention to the former disregard to the serious nature of complaints concerned with sexual harassment and sexual assault; especially, in the workplace. Still, there is reluctance on the part of male chauvinists to downplay such reprehensible conduct blaming women for consensual participation or claiming it's just the word of one party against the other.

Sexually harassing male supervisors often extort otherwise unwilling female subordinates with the loss of their jobs or the inability to rise higher in the organization.

The point of all the above is women have in the past and still are living under an alternate universe of unfair recognition. Although not as bad as in the past, the situation for men over women has and continues to result in a much easier path while attempting to navigate a world too often oblivious to recognizing the injustice of gender inequality.

SEVENTEEN

PAIRING OFF

Human circumstance is substantially influenced through the universal practice of pairing off. Obviously, humanity would cease to exist unless men and women got together to propagate its species. Marriage is the most common means for that to happen, but babies are born outside of marriage as well. Many couples live together outside of marriage and many couples live together with no intention of having children.

Same sex coupling within the hallowed halls of marriage or not is an increasing phenomenon. Unable to reproduce their own children, these couples often adopt thus extending their family line.

Whatever the means and motivation for pairing off, the result is that most humans end up in close personal relationships with others. Those who don't often develop close friendships that result in somewhat similar outcomes. Pairing off results in a slew of both positive circumstantial living benefits, but all too often some substantial negative outcomes as well.

The potential benefits of living together are numerous. Having someone to love and share common experience is often a determining factor in making life worth living. The joy of raising a family and all the additional benefits resulting therefrom are motivating factors for forging ahead in what might otherwise involve a life with far less meaning. The joy for grandparents as they share their lives with their ever-expanding posterity can't be matched in any other way etc. etc...

Living together involves people with different personalities, motivations, and views sincerely attempting to understand and accommodate each other's needs in the best of situations. Unfortunately, that kind of relationship too often doesn't exist, and a contentious rapport fosters all kinds of ill-fated consequences.

One of the worst consequences is spousal physical and emotional abuse. The circumstances surrounding the life of the one abused can spiral into a never-ending nightmare zeroing out any chance of experiencing a normal and satisfying life. With repetitive apologies and promises to change, the one abused extends the misery only to have the abuse repeated time after time. The worst result is serious injury or even death. But, even if that doesn't occur, too much of the life of the abused has been wasted when a prompt break in such a relationship might have resulted in the best outcome.

An unfaithful spouse can ruin a once blissful marital union. Although amends can be made and the relationship rekindled, too often such a tenuous relationship escalates into divorce and a contentious confrontation tearing a family apart and pretty much ruining the chance for family members to experience a normal and healthy life experience, a least for a period of time. Combative disputes often arise in relation to concerns like child custody and the division of marital assets.

We all know families were the children never cause a problem and grow up to be model citizens having achieved high grades in school and never coming close to becoming a parental burden of any kind. Good for those kinds of families. They're the lucky ones. Not every family ends up being so fortunate.

A problem child can turn the lives of parents and even grandparents into a vortex of worry and debilitating concern. Corruptible friends, drug use, low grades, and trouble with the law are just some of the fears that can distract from what otherwise might have been a pleasant and circumstantially satisfactory period of life. Although many wayward kids do eventually turn out ok, there are others that don't causing anxious unease never seeming to end for those who bore them.

I was fortunate that my five children all turned out well, although I went through a period of simi-agony getting there. I was a born worrier with good-looing daughters whose friends sometimes didn't meet the high standards I would have preferred. Some of the dating yahoos who landed on my front porch caused me no end of anxiety.

While most workers looked forward to weekends; for years, I dreaded them because that was when the inevitable dating, I so dreaded, kept me up late into the night when curfew was often ignored. The circumstances of my life during that worrisome period were less than optimum. The good thing about grandkids is I can enjoy them while their parents are tasked with any angst encountered in their raising.

I won't get into all the ups and downs concerning the relationship between brothers, sisters, uncles, aunts etc., but just state the obvious that the range of personal circumstantial relationships range all the way from loving livelong joyous bonds to complete disengagement for any number of contentious causes.

I'll close noting some of the problems I've observed with the death of one or both parents. When one dies, the remaining one often remarries often causing resentment by the children of both newlyweds. Monetary concerns too often arise when it comes to who gets what when a final inheritance is calculated.

Even when there is no subsequent marriage, there can be lifelong sibling recriminations about the division of assets following the death of the parents. Parents would be well advised to make their wishes crystal clear to prevent any such combative disagreements.

Whatever the results of the pairing off of humans, there can be little doubt the circumstances of the lives of all involved are substantially impacted.

EIGHTEEN

CHARITY

I would be remiss if I failed to include the role of charity has and continues to play in the lives of the misfortunate who for any number of reasons find themselves incapable of successfully negotiating life's numerous roadblocks.

Not all charitable efforts are created equally. Some are more philanthropically genuine than others. Before contributing to a charitable organization, I like to know exactly where my money is going to be applied. If most of it goes to enrich the organizers, I'm not interested. If the heads are paying themselves large salaries, that's not very charitable to me.

A list of the top worst charities to contribute to was put together by the Tampa Bay Times and The Center for Investigative Reporting based on federal tax filings for the last 10 years. Charities were broken up into five main categories: children, cancer, police/law enforcement, veterans, fire and other. These fifty charities accounted for more than $1.35 Billion in donations. Of that, $970 million went not to victims, but to the people who collected the money.

On the other hand, some of the best charities to donate to include The Salvation Army, Goodwill, ANVETS National Service Foundation and Habitat for Humanity. Significantly more of donations end up directly assisting those in need.

Comprehensive research is critical when attempting to rate charities. For example, although the exact motive is unclear, donations to the American Red Cross have been widely reported as claiming 92 cents of every dollar in donations ends up paying for administrative salaries. That's proven to be fiction. The truth is just the opposite. Charity Navigator, an independent website, rates thousands of charities. They've determined the Red Cross spends about 90 cents of every dollar on relief with only 10% going to cover administrative costs.

I have great respect for some of our fellow humans who are worth billions of dollars and who have committed to sharing their extreme wealth to improve the living circumstances of the ill-fated masses finding it difficult to survive the everyday trials unique to their station in life.

Wikipedia published the following recent list of the top 4 wealthiest charitable donations:

Rank	Organization	County	Endowment
1	Novo Nordisk Foundation	Denmark	$49.1 billion
2	Bill and Melinda Gates Foundation	U.S.	$46.8 billion
3	Stichting INGK A Foundation	Netherlands	$36 billion
4	Wellcome Trust	United Kingdom	$32.9 billion

Credible charitable organization fill a critical void in allowing the unfortunate to endure their treacherous sojourn in mortality. The survivable circumstances for those so aided can't be overemphasized.

NINETEEN

SCIENCE AND TECHNOLOGY

Intelligence was addressed in chapter 6. Taking it a step further, what humans with superior IQs have been able to accomplish are beyond my ability to comprehend. That's probably because my ability of achieving anything approaching even a small speck of their accomplishments is an absurd notion. Having so drastically improved the lives of humanity, they deserve the plaudits for all who have benefited which includes just about everybody. Certainly, they deserve special recognition in any analysis of the roots of human circumstance.

As a youngster, I remember being on our party line with a rotary dial to telephonically make contact with others; picking up the phone with somebody already talking, I would immediately hang-up and try again later. That particular daily circumstance has, of course, now taken a drastic turn for the better. I thoroughly enjoyed episodes of Dick Tracy in the comics and his ability to talk to others on his wrist watch even though I considered it total fiction at the time.

It doesn't seem that long ago that telephone booths with rotary phones were the only way to contact others outside the home. I haven't seen one of those for a long time now. Most everyone now has a cell phone and ready access to the internet. Gee whiz! Contact between humans residing in different countries takes seconds, an impossible reality only a few short decades ago.

It was only been in the 1960s in college where an assignment for a term paper required going to the card index platform at the library to try to identify books on the shelves required to address the topic I planned to pursue. Now I have, as does most everyone else, a computer with access to the internet to instantly obtain comprehensive information on any conceivable topic.

My TV watching was restricted to a small black and white that only played a few hours a day with severely limited quality programming. Now, I enjoy cable with dozens of channels and a plethora of movies to watch anytime I want. I'm able to watch all my favorite sporting teams without leaving my easy chair. How spoiled can you get?

Russia was first to have a man-made object touch the moon with its Luna 2 on 9/13,1959. I'll never forget on 7/20/1969 driving in my car with my radio on when I was totally flabbergasted and proud to learn America had successfully landed the first men on the moon on Apollo 11. I can't imagine the first humans looking up at the moon at night and having even the slightest inkling anything like that could ever happen. Will my kids live to see humans landing on Mars? I wouldn't bet against it.

The placement of hundreds of satellites rotating in outer space has affected all our lives in so many ways, the total benefit is difficult to tally.

I'm undoubtedly lucky to have been living for the last 18 years. My left anterior descending artery was clogged and would have likely resulted in a disabling and potentially deadly heart attack hadn't a stent been easily implanted to open up the flow. That procedure wasn't available not all that long in the past.

The development of life-saving drugs and the massive upward spiral of effective medical treatment has extended the lives and quality of life for billions of humans around the world. It's hard to come up with any other element of science and technology having a greater positive circumstantial impact on humanity.

Some argue science and technology have resulted in outcomes not all that rosy. For example, it's believed by many including myself we would have been better off had we not invented nuclear weapons of war. Many believe their use in bombing Japan wasn't necessary as they were close to surrendering anyway. Now, the extreme danger remains that unscrupulous terrorists could figure a way to someday initiate a barrage and utterly destroy the quality of life on earth.

I'm not all that fond of texting. It has been reported humanity has been programed by technology to constantly bury the faces of users in their cell phone to the extent beneficial personal contact and other more productive activities have been essentially set aside.

There are a few more complaints, but on the hole, science and technology have been a tremendous boon to civilization; arguably, unparalleled in how both continue to exponentially benefit the wide-ranging saga of human circumstance.

TWENTY

WAR

As a 2nd lieutenant in a mechanized Army infantry reserve unit in San Francisco, I came close being called up to go to Vietnam where the war was raging in 1967. I would have stood a decent chance of not returning alive or being disabled for the rest of my life. The only officers in my unit included a captain and two lieutenants, one of which was me. The captain was certain we were about to be called up and our week-end drills and two-week summer encampments at Fort Irwin outside Barstow, California were treated like we were fully engaged in combat.

Fort Irwin in the summer got up to 130 degrees. To toughen us up, we were required to sleep on the desert floor. Filling our canteens in the morning, the water was warm enough to shave with by noon. At the height of the daily heat, we were required to attack hills in armored personnel carriers with no air conditioning. Even soldiers returning from tours in Vietnam, required to attend a couple of extra summer camps, were being hauled off to the medical tent suffering from dehydration.

Luckily, I was able to transfer back to Utah to accept another job opportunity. I don't know if my company in San Francisco was ever called up. The point is that wars can and do pose a significant life or death threats encountered or avoided for those who end up or don't in the fray. The circumstances of humans can end up drastically different depending on the outcome.

Hesitant in over-emphasizing my life experience, I will anyway in referring to my experience in the military. Because of the draft and the fact reserve units weren't being called up at the time, I initially joined a Special Forces National Guard company in Utah. It ended up being a tough go from that point on. First, was basic training at Ft. Ord, California followed up by parachute jump school at Ft. Benning, Gregoria and finally Officer Candidate School. All three required confronting and overcoming challenging and difficult obstacles purposely intended to force me to drop out.

I'm convinced those tests I passed in the military helped me subsequently successfully navigate numerous challenging roadblocks of all kinds. That has allowed the circumstances surrounding my life to end up being far more fortuitus than had I not benefitted from the impediments I surmounted in the military.

On 5/27/2019, the Nation Magazine ranked the following U.S wars by the highest number of combatant deaths:

Rank	War	Years	Deaths
1	American Civil War	1861-65	498,332
2	World War 11	1941-45	405,399
3	World War I	1917-18	116,516
4	Vietnam War	1955-75	90,220

Most of those who died were in their late teens and early 20s. For decades thereafter, circumstances for good or bad that that might have otherwise been encountered were viciously and instantly abolished.

The above figures don't include the hundreds of thousands who were maimed including suffering from both physical and mental incapacities. The physical impairments like the loss of limbs are more obvious than the mental.

I worked alongside a Vietnam vet in Texas where we were both stationed as FBI Special Agents. He was the nicest and most considerate family man you could imagine, but he suffered from isolated bouts of depression and unexplainable anger.

Post-traumatic stress disorder (PTSD) results in trauma brought on from unwanted recollections of horror encountered in war. It includes nightmares, flashbacks, and occasional emotional instability making the lives of those so afflicted and those around them often difficult to navigate.

It's discouraging contemplating wars may apparently never cease to exist. At any one-time, warring factions are combating each other all over the world for any number of reasons. The death and surviving physical/mental toll for participants and those closest to them continues to explode with no end in sight. What a horrendous prospect!

TWENTY-ONE

FUN AND ENTERTAINMENT

By fun and entertainment, my intention is to include human activity outside the normal humdrum of daily life to include pursuits like hobbies, sports, entertainment, and similar refreshing diversions intended to make life a more enjoyable experience outside the more sobering every-day necessity of mere subsistence.

When I was about 12, my mom daily set the egg timer to 60 minutes insisting I learn how to read music and play the piano. At the time, I wasn't too thrilled with my friends free-wheeling it outside my window. I also played clarinet in jr. high. Later both those skills paid off big time in providing outlets making my life considerably more stimulating and gratifying.

I ended up playing tenor sax and leading a rock and roll band in high school. Later in life, I sang base in a semi-professional male rock and roll acapella quartet. One night, we were the opening act in Tyler, Texas for the then internationally famous Coasters. Every morning now, when I get up, I go to my Yamaha piano to start the day with a 30-minute practice session. I've just memorized six of my favorite Beetle tunes. Every day starts out on a high note (forgive the pun).

I'm fortunate my life experience has involved a continuing series of fun-filled challenges since my mom first turned the egg timer to 60 minutes. I pity those probably more talented, but for whatever reason, didn't pursue a similar path that could have resulted in the same kind of joy I've experienced.

Although following woefully short as being a draft pick or winning money in the pursuit of any sport, I did benefit from a healthy dose of extra-curricular sports in high school including being first string center for a short time on the basketball team and winning a doubles championship in tennis. Earlier, I was the first-string pitcher on my little league team. I played a lot of golf in the summers.

Those with wasted unproductive time are more prone to participate in detrimental activities leading to lifelong negative consequences. On the other hand, those who busily fill their extra time productively not only avoid harmful temptation, but gain an appreciation for fun and entertainment that will help yield a life filled with extra happiness and satisfaction.

Being able to temporarily escape the pressure of work and other mandatory responsibilities is both physically and emotionally liberating. Listening to one's favorite music or attending an exhilarating concert, cheering for a favorite sporting team while attending in person or watching on TV, crying through a touching movie on the big screen or cable TV are just a few examples of how the circumstances of everyday life can be made more bearable.

A challenging and enjoyable hobby can prove an important element in providing an exceptional life experience not otherwise obtainable. One I've considered at the top of the heap requires the skill of an artist. In retirement, I would have loved to have been able to spend hours converting artistic projects to canvas. Unfortunately, that's a skill that's inborn and can't be duplicated by those with the wrong DNA including myself.

For those humans unable to benefit from outside pursuits because they don't have the time or can't afford to pay the cost, it's a crying shame their lives won't be able to enjoy the solace and relief such pastimes provide. The circumstantial quality of their lives is most likely sadly inhibited.

TWENTY-TWO

INDOCTRINATION

Indoctrination has been described as altering the minds of others to accept the version of reality favored by the indoctrinator while purposely discouraging any views/facts to the contrary. It's often confused with education. The main difference is true education is objective while the last thing an unscrupulous indoctrinator wants is a critical analysis of the issues.

A destructive use of indoctrination is referred to as mind control. in which targets are exposed to the relentless mental programing over a period of time sufficient to cement the desired brainwashing intent. Often, without realizing the cleverly induced impact on their brains, targets slavishly accept the indoctrinated teaching refusing thereafter to acknowledge any contradictory input.

There can be little doubt indoctrination has and continues to play a large role in the circumstantial lives of humans. Adhering to indoctrinated infused beliefs obviously leads to life experiences that otherwise wouldn't have materialized. The preferable outcome in my opinion is to carefully analyze all sides of any teaching before making a final choice of what to believe. Objective scrutiny is the key to experiencing a life with eyes wide open.

Without meaning any offense to friends and family living exemplary lives due to their religious convictions, it's hard to ignore that all of organized religion has depended on controlling the minds of its base; especially, when it comes to indoctrinating members from an early age on. It's difficult not to be subjected to a hefty dose of brainwashing when the same dogma is permeated into the brain over a lengthy period of time.

I hypothesize devout Christians could end up equally devout Muslims having grown up in that culture. That's even though the doctrinal beliefs of each are diametrically opposed. It's not so much the dogma itself but the beliefs that have been continually buttressed into the brain; cemented to the point that any counter faith promoted by other religions is simply unworthy of any consideration whatever.

As alluded to in chapter 4, faith involving mind-controlled doctrine can and often does result in a positive outcome. That depends on the doctrines themselves. Living the golden rule, for example, results in a more satisfying and productive living environment for all involved. Many of the admonitions purported to have been expounded by Jesus have resulted in lives elevated to a higher standard of livability.

On the other hand, mind control can result is disastrous outcomes for gullible targets who have been expertly brain washed. Good examples are cults organized and led by evil charismatic charlatans. Past debacles include the Branch Davidians, Heaven's Gate and the People's Temple. Mind control was so successful as to unfathomably induce mass suicide. The brains of members were altered to the extent they felt no reluctance happily succumbing to the will of their beloved leaders.

Examples of cults still in existence include Scientology and NXIVM, although NXIVM's leader has been sentenced to a life in prison leaving fewer advocates in the wake.

Scientology was established by Ron Hubbard, a con-man with expertise in creating a large following while successfully promoting a phony sense of reality. After his death, the movement was taken over by David Miscavage, a ruthless indoctrinator, who bilked supporters of their assets based on nonsensical promotion strategies, separated family members, and made lives miserable for any who dared to defect.

NXIVM was led by an evil indoctrinator successful in isolating followers while brainwashing them to the extent they blindly fell into his trap of accepting whatever he wanted them to do completely counter to what they would have relented prior to their extended period of brain washing. Amazing, their minds had been so distorted they eventually succumbed to unthinkable extorted depravity including branding, rape and sex slavery.

One of the shorter examples of successful brainwashing occurred in 1973 in Sweden. Labeled the "Stockholm syndrome," bank robbers held four hostages for 131 hours after which they found themselves siding with the robbers. One of the four became engaged to a captor and another set up a legal defense fund.

Another highly publicized successful brainwashing incident occurred when Patty Hearst was kidnapped by the Symbionese Liberation Army in 1974. It took her quite a while to reverse her broken and complacent brain to its original state of mind. Experts caution it can take anywhere from a few weeks to several years depending on the circumstances of the brainwashing. Normally, the process of recovery can't begin until the victims on their own volition experience an "Ah- hah' moment.

Indoctrination, regardless of the level of severity, plays a major role in the lives of those who succumb; thus, triggering a full plate of negative circumstantial consequences that otherwise could have been avoided.

TWENTY-THREE

SEVEN DEADLY SINS

Although not a Christian myself, I think there's merit in examining the Christian tradition regarding the seven deadly sins including: lust, gluttony, greed, sloth, wrath, envy, and pride. There can be little doubt all seven can ominously impact human circumstance.

Lust is often thought of as seeking unrestrained gratification often related to sexual desire. It can ruin any semblance of a normal and productive lifestyle for those who succumb to the lack of control associated with this sin. The serial rapist is a prime example of unrepressed indulgence. The lives of victims can be scared for life. If caught, the perpetrator can count on spending most of his remaining years in a horrific custodial environment and forever being labeled a sexual deviant even if subsequently released.

Gluttony is normally referred to as the habit or act of eating too much. Although not always the case, it is often tied to those who are overweight. I hesitate to label overweigh individuals in general as sinful. That's because DNA if often responsible and it's unfair to criticize those who are genetically burdened no matter how hard they try to lose weight.

For the rest of us, gluttony is something we should be able to master with a concerted effort at self-control. Being overweight and unattractive means living a life that is not only unhealthy but results in a feeling of low self-esteem. Discrimination by others just adds to the burden.

Greed is defined in the dictionary as "wanting or taking all that one can get, with no thought of other's needs; desiring more than one needs or deserves." It doesn't refer to the healthy desire to improve one's station in life. It's going overboard and selfishly coveting more and more while disregarding any sense of a balanced life by ignoring other important sensible traits that should take precedence.

Charity can help rehabilitate a greedy heart by putting the desire to help others above storing up unending wealth for one's self. Many psychologists say they have witnessed more joy in life for those who concentrate more on helping others than trying to satisfy their own greedy cravings.

Sloth is often referred to as laziness induced by the disinclination to work or exert oneself. I doubt such apathetic indolence has anything to do with DNA. It's more likely something that most humans can control to better their lives. I suppose there are some contributing negative circumstances making it tougher for some than others. Poor parental upbringing and uninspiring teachers may be a couple of possibilities. Nevertheless, this is a failing most physical/mentally healthy humans should be able to overcome on their own and have no excuse for not doing so.

Wrath is a life altering human characteristic often associated with intense rage and frequently carried out in fits of unrelenting vengeance. Although not transforming into a vindictive criminal act of retaliation, I think I've often dabbled with wrathful thoughts. There are desires I won't identify out of fear of being visited by the Secret Service not to mention involving some dirty words. Let's just say the targets most recently sparking my wrath included former President Trump and Republican Senate Majority leader Mitch McConnel.

I think as long as you keep your wrathful thoughts to yourself and don't allow them to escalate into something stupid, wrath is a mostly harmless human trait not deserving to be included as a major source of severely damaging living circumstances.

Some actionable wrath can be minimized by making a concerted effort to put yourself in the shoes of those despised to discover some redeeming value for their despicable behavior. I tried that with Trump and McConnel to no avail. I still harbor unrequited wrath for both but with no desire for proceeding any further by harboring any vengeful/retaliatory motivation.

Envy is another one of the seven claimed sins I don't consider as all that destructive. It's hard not to covet a little over what others have that we can't afford. It's when that envy obsesses into uncontrolled jealousy and resentment that could better be converted to improving the reality of the economic situation we've been dealt.

Having a problem with excessive envy might be at least partially cured by concentrating more on helping those who have even less rather than fixating on matching those who have more. Certainly, a more productive and satisfying use of valuable time while seeking circumstantial stability.

Pride in one's accomplishments doesn't seem like a sin to me as long as it doesn't go too far. Too far to me is when it turns into an excessive view on one's worth with little regard for others. The worst result is narcissism and a lack of empathy. Boasting and bragging are other indications of going too far. Pride is something better maintained internally while refraining from arrogantly crowing of self-superiority.

TWENTY-FOUR

LONGEVITY

It's apropos to begin my final chapter around the human end game involving the longevity all of us are faced with like it or not. How long we're capable of living and the quality of life during that final portion of our lifespan determines the specific circumstances we'll end up encountering.

Some interesting hypothesizing: Dr. Cludia H. Kawas, Professor of Neurobiology and Behavior, University of California, theorizes half of the children born in 2020 in the United States and Europe "will reach their 103rd or 4th birthdays." In a study of those over 90, common traits include regular exercise, moderate drinking of alcohol and coffee, social engagement and putting on a few extra lbs. as we age.

At my maybe not so advanced age as I thought of 77, it has amazed me how the human body is capable of continuing to operate over such an extended period. With no electrical plug or source of battery power, the human heart continues to pump 24 hour/day year after year, an incompressible feat of durability. Of course, not everyone experiences the same resilience.

My mom and dad were inseparably joined at the hip in a marriage relying on their constant companionship to achieve their superlative circumstantial well-being. My dad died at age 65 while mom lived to be 93, Mom lived for 28 years with a circumstantial ache in her heart resulting in a cruel outcome from which she never quite recovered.

Depending on physical and mental health as longevity takes its toll, the question arises as to whether extended longevity results in a boon or a bust. Although dying at 65 like my dad would have prevented the joy and satisfaction I've enjoyed for the past 11 years, it was, at least, quick and instant with no extended incapacitating health issues needing to be endured. Mom, on the other hand, faced a plethora of unbearable health issues during her final extended years.

For those true believers who are convinced beyond a shadow of a doubt of the actuality of a heavenly after-life, I wonder why they wouldn't choose to exit mortality earlier than suffer through extended years of pain and suffering. And yet, it's not uncommon for most to choose living as long as possible regardless of the quality of life taking a nosedive. It makes me wonder just how sure they are about the reality of an eternal existence.

Personally, having lived a quality of life I wouldn't trade with anybody else; I'm prepared to cash out anytime now. That would probably result in missing some good still ahead, but might also preclude the possibility of suffering through problematic obstacles making life not all that worth struggling to hang onto.

I joke, but actually somewhat serious, the preferred circumstantial ending for me now would be to be in good health having just reached the final green on a round of golf, sunk a 30-foot putt, and suddenly collapse face down in the manicured grass from an aneurism having suffered no lengthy agonizing medical complications.

Well, enough of this disturbing topic. Let me conclude with a couple of unrelated final thoughts on my book in general.

Attempting to highlight all I deemed significant, I've tried to focus on some key root causes affecting the circumstances humans encounter throughout their lives. I'm sure readers can come up with some I've missed. Nevertheless, I hope I've raised awareness of the many triggers influencing our complex mortal reality.

I've thought it important to realize as soon as possible what we're facing in order to more easily recognize those obstacles we can head off at the pass before they bury our ability to respond. Looking back, I can now belatedly see how my circumstantial existence could have gone even smoother had I recognized and reacted to certain root causes confronting my particular life's journey.

Yes, there have been and always will be problematic roots mostly impossible to initially dodge such as inherited DNA, mother nature, and the station of life one is born into. But even those can be ameliorated and even reversed through concentrated individual determination and the help and cooperation of others.

My primary motivation has been for readers to be inspired to consider all the potential circumstantial roots they face and take decisive corrective action wherever possible to maximize all the upside and minimize inaction too often resulting in needless regret.